ABWW14

The Alamo Bay Writers' Workshop Anthology

2014

ABWW14

The Alamo Bay Writers' Workshop Anthology

2014

Introduction by Diane Wilson

Lowell Mick White, Editor

ALAMO BAY PRESS
SEADRIFT • AUSTIN

Cover Art: Reji Thomas
Photos: Pamela Booton / Sophie Rousmaniere / Kathryn Lane
Book Design: ABP

For orders and information:
Alamo Bay Press
Pamela Booton, Director
Lowell Mick White, Editor / Diane Wilson, Activist

825 W 11th Ste 114
Austin, Texas 78701
pam@alamobaypress.com
www.alamobaypress.com
www.alamobaywritersworkshop.com

Library of Congress Control Number: 2015909606
ISBN-13: 978-0-9908632-6-7

To the

Commercial Fishermen of Seadrift

Contents

ABWW14

The Alamo Bay Writers' Workshop Anthology

2014

Diane Wilson

Introduction: Inspiration at a Writing Workshop

That summer it was downright tedious living in Seadrift.

There was no one waiting at the docks and no one waiting to haul ice because there was NO ice at the fish house and NO one was catching anything. It was a do nothing time in a do nothing town.

Some fishermen said the docks were shutting down. Aww, the docks weren't shutting down. Anybody could see that, but the fish houses were for sure. Where, for instance, was Froggie's fish house? Bulldozed! And who did it? Well, wasn't none of anybody's business. Shrimpers were that kind of people. A trifle antisocial but who cared.

Well, the Alamo Bay Writers' Workshop did. And I was an instructor, so I did too.

The owner of the fishhouse who might loan us writing space was French. Or she had a French name. I didn't know which. I just talked to her over the phone and it was hard to tell. The dock cop who lived in a metal shack under a telephone pole gave me her phone number and said she was taller than him by a country mile and her skin was so white that she was sometimes mistaken for an albino witch when in fact she was just a plain jane gringo witch which wasn't a smidgen different from the Chicano La Bruja, the devil woman witch with pitch black hair that the Mexican deckhands claimed to see flying around Seadrift's docks late at night.

On the morning of the workshop, we ran late on everything because the French woman hadn't made up her mind and she wasn't in a big hurry to do that. At ten till our workshop, she did. That's when we found out the fish house had a piece of tin hammered across every window. It was hot as hell in that fishhouse so we sat marooned in the shade of an ash tree and drank Dr. Peppers by the case load. Well, at least I did. The rest of the writers drank bottled water that I had iced down in a ice chest that normally kept shrimp. The only comment that I got out of any of the writers was that the sun sure made them hot and the drinks cooled them down some. That's what they said, anyhow.

The writers worked their magic in front of waiting shrimp boats and every once in awhile a captain would holler at them, "What ya'll doin,' anyhow?" in a roundabout way, the shrimpers and the boats and the sun sliding up over our left shoulders helped the workshop magic along.

Inspiration.

That's the word.

At least that's how my story goes.

Not sure it's the same vanilla story they told.

Dorothy Ellis Barnett

Take a Chance

The spring I was seventeen, Bryon Tunnell Day in Tyler, Texas, 1963 was celebrated in the Rose Garden on the county fair grounds. I can't remember why Mr. Tunnell needed a celebration, but someone thought he did, but that's not important. Who was Bryon Tunnell? Texas Railroad Commissioner—but that's not important. What is important is that Francis Fix and a friend whose name has been lost to me invited me to go on a blind date with an "older" student who attended TJC (Tyler Junior College). What is important is that I had never been on a blind date before, had only been on three other dates, if you discount going to the movies with the gypsy boy when I was eight or nine. What is important is that on the night Bryon Tunnell was celebrated among thousands of roses blooming red, pink, yellow, white sweet scent hanging heavy in the air, I met my husband on a blind date. Someone asked me recently if I thought he had saved me—yes, he did and I saved him. We are still saving each other fifty years later.

Flip a Coin / Roll the Dice

How easy it has always been to think/wish myself away from my childhood. Easy to think that someone else could have adopted me, and my life would have been different/better. My life could have been decided by flipping a coin. Heads I go to live with Laura and Kenneth, tails I'm sent along another path. Recently my oldest daughter found Mary and Frank—Laura and Kenneth's friends at the time of my adoption. After telling me that Frank had taken his own life right in front of her—shot himself with a shotgun —gore ever where, Mary's voice over the phone became the raspy voice of too many cigarettes and too much whisky as she said, "I almost took you, but Kenneth and Laura wanted a baby, so I let them have you." Flip a coin/roll the dice, how simple.

Linda Caplin

Only A Moment Ago

Dedicated to my son, Jason,
on his 50th birthday: March 24, 2015

It was only a moment ago that I held you in my arms for the first time. Your blue, blue eyes had the longest eyelashes I'd ever seen on a baby!

It was only a moment ago you put on your little policeman's uniform your Gramma had given you and you came in the living room to watch *Adam 12.* Then you ran back in your room to change into your cowboy clothes—*Gunsmoke* was coming on! You climbed on your trusty horse, Shy Anne, and rode off with Matt Dillon and the others. Prompting our neighbor to say, "Does Jason have any real clothes or just costumes?"

It was only a moment ago when you sat on the desk in the dining room while your Dad and I told you we were getting a divorce. Your sad little face still haunts me.

It was only a moment ago you and your little sister were getting off the plane in Florida, each dressed in your cowboy clothes from Tiny's Western Wear. Boots, fringe suede jackets and cowboy hats. You clutching Julie's hand and in the other, your loyal companion, Pooh Bear.

It was only a moment ago that you called me from Dallas and said Mommy, I left Pooh Bear on the bus! I know I'm too old to carry him with me but he's my best friend. Lori called Greyhound and asked them to look out for a bear traveling alone. The bus company called and said they found a bear who looked very loved.

It was only a moment ago when you told me you were joining the Army National Guard right after you graduated from high school. You, Matt, and Hugh went off to boot camp at Fort Knox. Later, you switched to the Air Force Reserves saying, "Who dies in the Army? Everyone! Who dies in the Air Force? Pilots!"

It was only a moment ago that I moved to St. Louis to go to grad school and try to salvage my marriage to Barry. You and Tessy had split up, and you moved into the Pearce's garage apartment. When you were bemoaning my moving, I said, "Jay, you know you would have to leave the nest some day." And your reply was an arrow to my heart, "Yes, but I didn't think the nest would leave me."

It was only a moment ago when you picked me up for Christmas vacation, and announced, I've good news and bad news. Good news is Betty and I got married today. Bad news I'm being deployed very soon to Desert Shield. So I ordered a cake from HEB with one section decorated with a Bride and Groom, one with a diploma, and one with palm trees and fighter planes!

It was only a moment ago that you became a father, first with Ryan, and a year and a half later, with Jon. You said, "Mom, I love Ryan so much, how can I ever love Jon as much?" I said, "Oh, Jay, you will."

It was only a moment ago that you called and said, "Well, the rhythm method doesn't work." And a few months later Mackenzie was born.

It was only a moment ago that you were called to duty again for Operation Enduring Freedom. Then you returned home seemingly healthy but that didn't last.

It was only a moment ago you developed pancreatitis and you were hospitalized for over two months—two weeks in an induced coma—before you got well. We were so afraid you'd die. But instead you gave instructions to your surgeons! One said, "Jay, your insides look like an old man ready to die, but your outsides are telling me what to do and how to do it. You just keep that attitude, let me do my job and well get through this."

It was only a moment ago that I took such great joy in being MeeMa to your boys and now Mackie, and I have such pride in your accomplishments. Lieutenant with the Travis County Sheriff's Department, Master's Degree in the Air Force, Lt. Colonel in the Air Force, and always being a great family man.

But now you are 50 and ready for AARP, while I still see the darling tow-headed curly-haired little boy who became my son.

Only a moment ago!

Linda Dane

Birds

Inspired by a bird in Janie's Garden
"Written on the Fly"

I dream of birds

I dream of cardinals dotting the snow in winter
and squads of pelicans over the bay.

I dream of parrot Charlie Bird kissing my cheek and
murmuring, "I love you."

I dream of cranes and flamingos with their long legs
and slow moving grace.

I dream of islands of rosy roseate spoonbills
and summer mockingbird songs.

I want to fly.

Gracie Fleming

Druid in Black Leather

The birds were talking to me. Their messages were clear although not decipherable in a rational kind of way. They didn't speak to me because I was special. It was simply that I could tune in to their wavelength.

This particular day in 2007 didn't start with avian communion. It wasn't until my car broke down that I stopped to listen and watch and accept that I was part of a much larger existence.

"Murphy's Garage." The man's voice with its Central Texas twang traveled through the ether into my cell phone with a promise of help.

"John, this is Grace. I drive the 2000 Maxima. I just got out of a meeting and I'm trying to get back to my office, but the car won't start. When I turn the key it acts like it's going to start but it doesn't."

"Does the engine turn?"

"Yeah. But nothing else."

"Where are you? I'm gonna have a truck come pick up the car. You can ride back with him, if you want, and we can give you a ride to work."

Relief washed through me. "If you'll just get the car, that'd be good. Bernard has a break between clients, he can come get me."

My black wool jacket absorbed the bright sun to heat my back and shoulders on that chilled winter day. I welcomed its warmth. I had some time before Bernard arrived. I allowed myself to simply relax, enjoy my surroundings and think about my friend Alex, who was facing cancer and trying to take care of her infant daughter. I knew cancer up close and personal. I knew the fear Alex faced and the courage she needed.

I stood in a parking lot in a place that still felt like the edge of the city. A metal recycling center was the closest neighbor. A drive to the east quickly became country with lots of trees and native grasses keeping distance between houses. To the west was the old airport that developers had converted into a mixed-use neighborhood with housing and retail, a children's hospital, and office buildings. Across the street, trees filled empty lots on rolling hills for as far as I could see.

I gazed at the tree-filled hills and thought about Alex. She received her breast cancer diagnosis only a few weeks after her only child was born. That took me back to my own diagnosis twelve years earlier and just two weeks after marrying Bernard. The fear, raw and shocking like the touch of a frayed electrical cord, consumed waking hours and sleep alike.

A few minutes later, I laughed out loud. It was safe to laugh out loud alone. There were no people nearby. I thought about Bernard. He had been there for me through the cancer surgeries and radiation and chemotherapy. We had been there for one another struggling to build a life from the ruins of our families. Pain and struggle threaded their way throughout our marriage, but we managed somehow to carve out a life together. Now I was stranded on the edge of town and he was coming to get me. I heard him coming before I saw him. A thicket of live oaks adorned grass covered hills, beyond which the road rose and curved to block my view. But, I heard him. His motorcycle rumbled when he slowed for that bend and then it yelled a war cry as he picked up speed before slowing again at the entrance to the complex where I waited. All I could do was laugh. My knight in shiny armor on a white stallion was in fact a druid in black leather and wraparound shades on a motorcycle. It was appropriate. We were meant to be together.

He made a tight circle around me, turned off the engine and got off the motorcycle. He peeled off his black leather gloves. "D'they get the car already?"

"Yeah. They just left about five minutes ago."

He gave me a kiss and said, "D'you have gloves? You're gonna need to wrap that scarf better. Cover your neck."

"I didn't bring gloves. It's a nice day. And this scarf isn't really warm. It's just decoration."

"Well, it's better than nothin." He turned to rummage through one of the saddlebags and withdrew a pair of work gloves for me. He pulled off his helmet and handed it to me. My generation was the last one where men would give women their jackets when it was unexpectedly cold. Still, my man was not going to give up that leather jacket knowing how the cool air became frigid while sailing along on a bike. But, if there was only one helmet, he wanted me to be the one to wear it.

While I readied myself for the refreshing ride I was about to take, he told me where we would be going. "I need to drop something off south. And I'm on my lunch break anyway so we should go get some lunch. D'ya feel like La Reina?"

I loved the double entendre of that question. La Reina was a great Tex Mex restaurant in South Austin. I had been eating there since I came to Austin in 1983. Their food was much like what we ate on the border where I grew up. So I stood there in the black cherry helmet, the rearranged scarf, and huge men's work gloves, thinking about La Reina. The phrase literally means The Queen. It is also used to refer to Mary, as in Jesus' mother. So when, I said, "Yes." I really did feel like La Reina. Queen of goofy, maybe, but a queen nonetheless.

We put my office bag in one of the saddlebags and off we went. As soon as we picked up speed on the road, I found myself pressing close to Bernard's back. The cold wind bit our cheeks and whipped our thighs and exhilarated us. This was the reason he rode a motorcycle. We were on a machine but we were in a relationship with our surroundings. We flew down the road into the city and across the river.

On South First Street we headed toward the restaurant. Traffic was slower and the wind not as sharp. We approached the building where Alex had her office as a psychotherapist. Suddenly, I knew I had to look up. That was no small feat while wearing a helmet and balancing on the back of a moving motorcycle. I had to sit up straight, away from the shelter of Bernard's wind blocking back.

When I managed to look up, I saw a red-tailed hawk high overhead with wings and tail beautifully spread. It swept the air flying in circles that looked peaceful even though I knew it was probably scouting for a meal. I remembered the day I finished chemo.

For six months, I had gone to chemotherapy every other week. It was grueling.

Cancer treatment was almost a year long, stretching from September of 1995 to June of 1996. In October, I began thirty-eight radiation treatments. Thirty-eight times I waited my turn to lie under a machine shooting me with radiation while everyone evacuated the room. Thirty-eight times I watched other patients, waiting their turns or skipping ahead of the line in wheelchairs to keep us waiting longer. Thirty-eight times I watched other cancer patients withering or enduring and I wondered how much I would wither before all of the treatments were ended. I watched my fellow patients and I knew who was active in the process of dying. With radiation over, I began chemotherapy. Six months of chemotherapy.

Two weeks on and two weeks off, that was the regimen. I had two weeks of chemo and then spent two weeks trying to rebuild my blood count so that I could tolerate the next round. My strength drained with my blood cells. That state-of-the-art treatment in the art of medical science to me felt barbaric. Boosting my blood count caused as much pain as anything they did to me. One injection delivered a great discomfort so deep in my bones I just wanted to cry. But it was one of those pains made worse by sobbing so I simply lay down on the bed, holding silence and stillness.

After six months, that last treatment was monumental. Bernard came to the clinic after I was already hooked up to the drip in a small room in the clinic that was about a mile from our house. Chemo was always on Friday and whether Bernard was able to join me or not, we always went to Furr's Cafeteria afterward, where we could get a well balanced meal of our choice without the smell of food permeating our house and making me sick. That final treatment warranted one more meal at the cafeteria and so we decided to drop off one car and drive together to Furr's.

I followed Bernard out of the parking lot onto the road, and I saw a red-tailed hawk overhead. I lost sight of the bird as the trees thickened. As soon as we made the first turn toward our neighborhood, again the bird sailed above in the same straight line we traveled. The three of us made three more turns together before reaching our driveway. As I got out of the car, I caught one last glimpse of the harbinger hawk. I gave thanks. I had gained weight and lost strength with the barbaric science, but what meant the most at that moment was this message from the Universe. This exclamation point of the spirit world in the form of a hawk! Hawks signify extraordinary senses and the power to make intentions reality. A hawk had played a role in a novel I had been writing. For me, hawks also mean freedom to create and the ability to see the world from a unique vantage point. That hawk had a message for us. Treatment was done and so was cancer. It was time to move forward.

Bernard pretty much jumped out of the car and turned to me with a smile. "Did you see the hawk? A red tail!"

I laughed. "Yeah. It brought us home."

Now trying to balance on the back of the motorcycle while looking up at the sky over Alex's office, the Universe told me, "It will be okay. She will watch her daughter grow up."

I celebrated that news with a plate of chicken mole at La Reina. I celebrated the fact that I had grown up with a culture that allowed me to recognize the place of nature and spirit in everyday life. And I celebrated my druid in black leather.

Lee Meitzen Grue

I Miss the Ships

Many things gone with our parting
I do not miss
your sense of ownership.

Certain freedoms not mine
maintained for your secret pleasures
laughing up your sleeve in happy guilt and ego.

I do miss the ships
those behemoths
sailing through our marriage.

The ports I heard you anchored
I did not sail to:
Grand tales.

Captains you teased and challenged.
Fathers you emulated
as a lowly Third Mate.

The dirty ports and easy lovers
you took as rite of passage.
I, the reader of swashbuckling tales,

allowed you without question as
the second-hand adventures I enjoyed
landlocked you, given up for treasure.

I do not miss
unwanted gifts you brought home
from other beds than mine.

I do miss the ships.

God of the Dream

some are dead on the bottom
voices swim between
i'm way up here
god of the dream

sometimes a thunderbolt

details escape me
earthquakes and hurricanes
nightmares
are their domain

there is little connection
between artistic direction
and
the full blown dream

a dream is hard to keep track of
wildly ungovernable
lacks control
craves love

old voices
complain
blind need
wants a mother

let me tell you

being a god
is not all it's
cracked up to be.

Brasil: Itaparica

I, as usual, choosing to stay at sea,
viewed the island from a distance
rocking on a swell slightly off shore. There
lives
someone to greet me,

call my name,
but I doze on a clean ship slightly off shore,
my gaze caught by the ship's wheel
rolling
with the waves.

Anchored, free of guidance or hindrance
like that other sleepy castle
our crew rests lazily atop the boat's cabin.
We rock in freedom no master here.

Sky and beach afar
where music plays faintly
too distant for the tune.
On shore, racing horses,
ridden by faceless riders.

The sand immaculate.
The mountain climbable.
All possibility with no charge or hire,
as I rock dreamily on a boat at sea
somewhere near Heaven and Brasil.

At the Bogalusa Blues Festival

A man stood
between me and the stage
emptying a garbage can.
He wore black and white prison stripes.
Prison garb
all day
on a day the sun shone, flags waved, and music
bound musicians to us.
A place where music flowed into us and around us
and the grass was greener than green
as the jail house trustees
emptying cans
wore their shame as a public rebuke.

Their shame, our shame
at the time
Ruthie Foster sang Ring of Fire,
as a slow hymn to the sky.
She sang, "I fell into a burning ring of fire
and the flames rose higher"
and it was still about desire, ours
and the man in the prison suit
between me and the stage
reminding me how easy it is to fall.

How freedom is hard to maintain
in Bogalusa, a town
the poet Yusef Komunyakaa

came from,
where his picture now reigns supreme
on a wall
among their favorite sons,
reminding me once more:
the blues
are always with us.

My Old Cat

I would like a young cat,
a young cat,
to pet beside the fire,
if I get a young cat
my old cat might die.

My old cat is a bean bag,
when I pick her up
all of her middle
runs to her front.

Incredibly dirty,
she slouches 'round the house,
triumphs over evil,
as she strikes the skulking mouse.

My old cat is uppity,
she never sits in laps,
but if a person's full of tears she'll
kindly lend her back.

Her opinion of house dogs
is really rather low,
she has lived 18 years
and always seen them go.

I would like a young cat,
a young cat

to play silly games,
I would like a young cat
to comfort and amaze.

If I get a young cat
my old cat might die.
I would lose the deep dreams
in the dark seams
of her yellow eyes.

Gina Harlow

Hot Seat

In the swampish air I steep like a soggy teabag. In the company of cars and trucks, with gravel and shell under foot, I sit by the bay. Pen and paper in hand, I watch my fellow fledglings gather. Others who, like me, have a need; a pull subtle or strong to write it down. Feet away, the shrimp boats rest in the harbor. Their long black nets hang like mourning veils from their riggings, and they, too, look wilted. But like all boats, they are splendid as they shine in the sun. They, like us, are a group of storytellers with much to confess.

Little is said as people find seats wherever they can. But amidst the occasional grind of the engine and the squawk of gulls overhead there is question and anticipation. Why this place? I remind myself that I chose this coastal town, obscure and treasured only by its inhabitants, to come to draw with words a picture, or a succession of pictures. Now, in it's crustiest corner, I sit hoping to be filled. But hoping, too, that in these crude surroundings I will receive it quickly.

The back of my legs cling with sweat to the hard plastic chair. Waiting, my mind wanders, and I remember last summer and the gentle suggestion of the young gratingly serene girl who lead my yoga class. Be comfortable with the discomfort, she said. That was in a pretty park by the Pacific. And it did hurt, that day in the cool mist and green grass. In the end, the strained movement woke muscles I knew nothing of as they came alive with pain. I could see them in my mind's eye, long and sinewy and as attractive as painted lips. As I moved an arm or lifted a leg I could visualize their elegance, stretched around bones and tendons. It was something I could only know in misery.

Back in the parking lot, I hear the writing teacher. She tells us that it is here on the pavement, in the petroleum scented smell of decaying sea life, chosen in particular for its lack of allure, that we will pull forth anything worth saying.

Now write! Be done in five minutes!

The blank page in my lap taunts me with its whiteness. I consider escape and spy the faces of my fellow composers. I see confusion on some, and watch as others begin to scribble. Then, the ticking clock commands me to the edge. It's time, my turn. A voice from somewhere that only I hear says, Go!

Write like it hurts. Write like I kicked you, or kissed you. Tell me, the voice seemed to say.

What I wrote was only a scrap and not a story. It was about my mother and about loss that was still fresh. With no time for honing, it was rough in a way that a newly mined gem is course and smudged, but genuine and with glimmers of brightness, and it was pulled from a place deep within me.

I know now I was brought to that shore not to be comforted or reassured, but to understand the telling of truths. In my discomfort, I found something worthy of pronouncement. Maybe what I found were questions, but questions that needed asking, that in cozy surroundings, I might not have posed. I pinched myself and wrote what came. Quick and unrefined, it was primal. In a kind of agony, I spoke out of reflex, in a voice as unique as my fingerprint, and told of what I know as only I can. Anything less, I learned, is better left unsaid.

Julie J. Johnson-Jones

Telephone Operator: I Wrote It For You

Just yesterday, it seems like two years; I was calling New York, and I had a few fears.
I'd been working all day, just dialing my phone; I'd started to think like that damn busy tone.
Off and on, off and on, that's all I ever heard; Then it started to ring, and all you said was one word.
You weren't the wife, that was easy to see; the husband, I thought, how lucky could she be.
So I decided to play this, with a little bit of fun; Thats when I found out that you were their son.
So red in the face, and as embarrassed as could be; I said I was sorry, it was the first time you see.
We laughed a few times, then you started to talk; I wished my bosses, would take a long walk.
When we finally said goodbye, it was sort of hard to do; See I'm not great at goodbyes and neither were you.
That night while in bed, I recapped my day; and all of a sudden, I had so much to say.
So that's when I decided exactly what to do; so I wrote this poem especially for you.
In Texas, roses are yellow, and violets aren't blue; but this poem is original because I wrote it for you.

My Soldier

His love was passionate and full of lust; as he held me tight and caressed my bust.
A Soldier Never Looks Back.
He took a shower and kissed me goodbye; when he walked out the door all I could do was cry.
A Soldier Never Looks Back.
He said "remember my face as you see it now, for when I return you can't ask me how."
A Soldier Never Looks Back.
He joined his friends who waited close by; I prayed to the lord that he would not die.
A Soldier Never Looks Back.
They entered the alley where it all took place; sure there was fear, but it's something they had to face
A Soldier Never Looks Back.
A gun went off and his friend went down; he kept on walking without a sound.
A Soldier Never Looks Back.
The picture stayed within their minds; the blood, the drugs, and guns of all kinds.
A Soldier Never Looks Back.
Seven to five, and then to four; that meant he had to even the score.
A Soldier Never Looks Back.
Just once he did; he thought about her love. That's when the last guy shot from above.
My Soldier Should Have Never Looked Back...I am burying my soldier today!

Music Man

You caress your Axe, just like you hold me;
soft and gentle,
the way music is supposed to be.
Note for note, the way you play;
your music has meaning,
so much to say.

M - is for the MEANING, that you put in every song.
U - is for the UNDERSTANDING, that you have all day long.
S - is for SINCERITY, so genuine and true.
I - is for INFATUATION, a feeling I have for you.
C - is for CULTURE, that you added to my day.
M - is for the MYSTERIOUS, things that you say.
A - is for APPRECIATION, the gratitude I have for you.
N - is for NEGLECT, something you sometimes do.

When it comes to music, I fall to second place; but its okay,
when I see your smiling face.
It makes it worth, the hell I go through; to hear you play a
song or two.
So Music Man, remember these things; I love you as much
as you love your strings.

True Love

True love you will be easy, to forget you will be hard;
To need you isn't a gamble, for you're the winning card.

True love is what I'll call you, to brighten up my day;
To hold you in my awaiting arms, is not that far away.

To love me is a blessing, to hold me long and true;
To have me in your beating heart, will be my gift to you.

True love we have a future, together we'll make it be;
To ride into a life with you, is a future I want to see.

Dedicated to my husband. This one was written down in Seadrift, while lying in bed thinking about being away from my husband. I just hated being away from him, even for that short time.

Diane Kramer

Observations on Nature

A fast *twit, twit, twit* sings the window screen as a goldfinch with yellow underbelly plucks gnats from their wire mesh prison. The pale white of early dawn fans the sky behind the tiny bird's feast. Crows *caw caw* lazily as pink and coral begin to burnish the clouds, signaling the sun's rise for another day. Mourning doves sit shoulder to shoulder on a nearby power line and coo softly as the air begins to heat these early hours and dries last night's dew from their wings. Cardinals and meadow larks flit among barren tree branches, looking like red and golden baubles on a Christmas tree long ago abandoned or perhaps school children in brightly colored sweaters swinging on playground equipment, the winter wind a partner on their teeter totter.

******

An early morning cloud hangs low in the trees taking its rest on the barn roof, a ghost shadow of something not seen or not remembered. In tandem with fog on the nearby pasture, black vultures roost on the branch of a dead tree and conjure up a long ago Halloween.

*****

With tails and ears twitching lazily, a group of female deer graze beside the fence line. The large doe turns and holds her head erect like a sentry on heightened alert, then stamps the ground with her hoof, signaling danger to the others. They ignore her, too busy with their breakfast. She stomps again, then again. In soundless unison they turn and bound across the fence, white tails whipping side to side as flags in a strong breeze. They disappear across the dry creek to the hay pasture leaving behind a trace of scent to tell others that happen by that here lies the spot where she'd seen a predator.

*****

A dirt road stretches down a high ridge, following the property lines of several ranches. Its isolation creates safe passage in the dark of night for many creatures, from one side to the other, hay meadow to creek. An early morning walk reveals the previous night's visitors. A pad with four toes and no claw marks signals a bobcat traveled that way, various sizes and directions the only remains of a group, perhaps a female with cub. Two-toed hooves, small and pointed, others large and rounded, tell others that both deer and feral hogs use the route, too. Another pad with four toes, this one with claw marks is canine, most likely coyote. Their late night yips usually come from this distant direction. Soon the sunlight dances on the brown fur of a coyote carcass lying in the ditch. As each day goes by, his body morphs from distended belly to merely leathered skin and tufts of fur, eyes missing, fangs extending from the grimace of its mouth. The vultures have done their work, even back paws are chewed off.

*****

A tiny calf steps gingerly through the bones of an unknown ancestor scattered across the field in a feeding frenzy by coyotes, then vultures, only its mother mourning the loss of one of her own. The herd turns in unison as the woman approaches, their faces wary and curious. A few grunt or snort, one bellows, the young ones gamble to their mama's side and nuzzle her underbelly for a nourishing and comforting teat.

*****

Two vultures pull and tug at something invisible on the dry yellow grass, a third dismissed to the side, waits a turn. Wings flap and bump each other as beaks yank entrails from the body for a delicious meal. It doesn't last long. Upon inspection, only bits of fur remain, no bones or toes or claws to identify whose life was lost. Human eyes see bright red blood smeared about and dotted with tufts of brown and gray, a touch of a finger senses evenly soft fur. Far off to the side lies a small white cotton tail.

Kathryn Lane

My Daughter's Hand

"Call up all your good customers and tell them to come on over for a tequilazo to celebrate Sofía's engagement. I want it to be a night to remember," Pancho said. "It's not every day a man's youngest daughter gets engaged."

Nacho, the bartender and owner of Nacho's Cantina, looked contemplative as he listened to his friend Pancho.

"If Sofía has only known the novio for three months, why are you so enthused about the wedding?" Nacho asked. "Don't you want to get to know him better before Sofía marries him?"

"Listen, Compadre, you have to hit while the iron's hot, as they say. Get them hitched mientras el muchacho tiene ganas. You never know when a guy might change his mind."

"Yeah, but have you checked this gringo out?" Nacho asked. He cleaned the top of the bar with a damp cloth. "He's from New York City. What's he doing in New Mexico? You don't know him well enough. Besides, Sofía is a beautiful young woman. She's had lots of pretendientes right here, suitors among the sons of families you've known all your life. Are you sure this gringo is the right guy?"

"Listen to me, Nacho. El muchacho tiene dinero and a good job. What else does Sofía need?"

"Money's not everything" Nacho said. "Más vale malo por conocido que bueno por conocer. No matter how good things seem at first, it's best to know people for a while before letting them into the family."

"Listen to me, Nacho, call up your friends and

customers. I tell you this will be a night to remember," Pancho said.

◆

The bar, noisy and boisterous, was full of people when Jim Hudson arrived. Pancho, a shot glass of tequila in hand, swaggered over to welcome Jim. People were already drunk or getting there, including Pancho.

"Hey, everybody," Pancho said. "This is my future yerno." He slurred his words as he held his glass up to toast his future son-in-law. He put his arm around the young man. Pancho looked around the room, full of men, mostly middle aged or older. He'd known all of them most of his life. His drinking buddies all held up their shot glasses to make a toast.

"This is Sofía's novio," Pancho said. "Felicidades al novio. He's taking my little girl, the last of my fifteen children. I invite all of you to the wedding." Pancho held back the tears as he finished the toast. He took a bright red bandana-type handkerchief from his pocket. He dried his eyes and blew his nose.

Nacho stood behind the bar, pouring shot glasses of tequila for those who wanted to toast again.

Lalo, a short, wrinkled-faced old man wearing a Mexican sombrero, came forth and stood next to Pancho.

"Salud, mi compadre Pancho," Lalo said. "I want to toast to your virility. Ya eres un viejo. If you were not so old, you and Marina would still be making babies."

"Hold what you say, mi compadre Lalo. I can still father children," Pancho said. "It's my wife who's too old."

Lalo stepped to the front of the group, in front of the bar, and faced the crowd.

"I propose a toast to Marina and to Sofía. They're not here so I'll represent them," the crusty one said. "It's Marina who raised the kids and kept Pancho out of trouble. Here's to Marina."

"Para Marina. Salud. Salud," the crowd shouted. The gathered group of fifty or more were all standing, clinking shot glasses and slapping each other on the back.

Lalo, the compadre, cleared his throat. "Marina is a saint. I want to toast to her sainthood, a saint who puts up with this viejo pendejo," Lalo said.

Pancho staggered over to Lalo and punched him in the mouth. "You're the pendejo idiot. Why do you keep making toasts to my wife?" Pancho demanded. "Are you in love with her? Eres un puto, and I thought you were my friend." Pancho took another swing at Lalo but missed, lost his balance and fell to the floor.

Jim rushed over to help Pancho up. It was an effort for Jim to get Pancho off the floor.

Nacho stopped tending bar and took an empty wine bottle by the fat end and used the narrow end as a baton.

"Atención amigos, atención. Vamos a echarle porras al novio." He waved the wine bottle and started the cheer.

Chiquita bum bum bum
Te casas con la más bella
Quien sabes
Pero la linda es ella
Chiquita bum bum bum
Chiquita bum bum bum

By now Pancho was standing again. He knew Jim's Spanish was limited, so he tried to translate the cheerleading song.

"Don't worry, Pancho. I understood everybody is cheering my beloved as the beautiful one and not me," Jim said. "I can speak a little Spanish. I'm not just a New Yorker. I'm a New Mexican now." He danced to the jig and drank a full shot glass of tequila straight down. And then another tequila. And another.

Pancho slapped Jim on the back and nearly fell over doing so. Jim grabbed his future father-in-law to hold him steady.

"Órale, hold yourself up," Jim said.

"You're learning Spanish fast," Pancho said.

"Pos, sí, I speak muy bueno Spanish," Jim said. He and Pancho clicked glasses and downed the tequila Nacho had just served them.

"Before I pass judgment on this marriage, I mean, before I consent...before I give you my daughter's hand...."

Pancho stopped. His voice was breaking up. He took his bandana handkerchief out, wiped his watering eyes and blew his nose. He tried to put the handkerchief back in his pocket but missed and it fell to the floor.

"Now, where was I?"

"Standing right here in Nacho's bar giving me permission to marry your daughter," Jim said. He bent over to pick up the handkerchief and felt buzzed himself.

"Where is that son-of-a-bitch pendejo who said my wife is a saint?" Pancho asked. He looked around the room. He spotted Lalo and staggered over to him, holding on to the backs of several chairs as he walked. "You know, you're correct. My wife is a saint. I don't deserve her." Pancho took his handkerchief out again and wiped his eyes.

Pancho looked at Lalo, deciding if he should hit Lalo again or not. Pancho thought about it for a minute and extended his hand to Lalo. The two old men shook hands.

"We've been compadres all our lives, so let's be friends again," Pancho said. He hiccupped. "Oye, Nacho, bring me another tequila to celebrate my friendship with Lalo." He saw Jim standing near the bar and waved at his future son-in-law to join him. "Now where was I?"

"Giving me permission to marry tu hijo," Jim said.

"No, no, I think you want to marry my daughter Sofía, not one of my sons. My sons are married anyway. One of them married his boyfriend in California. Nice boy, you know."

"Casarme yo con Sofía," Jim said.

"Right's right. Uh, that's right. So let's talk business," Pancho slurred. "It's an old Spanish custom for the couple to have padrinos, padrinos for the ceremony." He signaled Nacho to serve him another tequila which Pancho wasted no time in drinking.

"Padrinos?" Jim asked.

"Yeah, yeah, they help pay for the wedding and they are your...well, what should I call them?" Pancho asked.

Nacho, by now the only sober person in the bar, came to Pancho's rescue. "Padrinos are usually an older, married couple who act as marriage counselors or spiritual advisors for the young couple. They also put the lazo around the bride and groom at the marriage ceremony."

Pancho sat down and put his head on the table. He still held the empty shot glass in his hand.

"Whew, wait a minute, I'll pay for my own wedding," Jim said. He swayed back and forth. "If a man gets married, he has to support his woman. I can do that. Don't need anyone else paying. Don't need marriage counselors telling us what to do, either. I know what to do."

The whole room laughed with Jim and they all held up their shot glasses for another porra.

> ¡Qué viva el novio! ¡Qué viva la novia!
> ¡Qué tengan tantos hijos como la lluvia!
> ¡Chiquita bum! ¡Chiquita bum!

When the room quieted down, Nacho pulled Jim aside and whispered in his ear. "Padrinos are good to have. You can pay for everything and they can be symbolic but you need them for the lazo."

"All right, all right, we'll have padrinos. What's this thing about roping us with a lazo?" Jim asked. He used his hand to show his neck being squeezed. He careened as he mimicked the rope around his neck. He reached out to grab a table to hold himself up.

"That's also pure symbolism. It's a large double rosary the padrinos put around you to show you and Sofía are united for life and all eternity," Nacho said.

Pancho raised his head off the table. He looked at Jim with bleary eyes. "Don't forget to buy the arras. Thirteen gold coins...."

Pancho's compadre Lalo, still wearing his Mexican sombrero, turned to face Jim. "You'd better get real gold coins and not gold plated ones. Sofía deserves the best."

"Don't say that about the arras," Pancho said. "I know Jim will buy good stuff for his bride. Just look at my future son-in-law. He's a financial advisor. He and Sofía will make good children, too." Pancho scratched his head. "You and Sofía will give me grandchildren, right?" Pancho started crying. He took his red bandana handkerchief out again and wiped his eyes.

"Of course we'll have children." Jim said. "But not right away."

"Let's talk finances," Pancho said. He wiped his eyes again and blew his nose. He put the handkerchief in his lap and it fell onto the floor. "It's an old Spanish custom for the novio to show his intent to support his bride by buying a lamb and giving it to his suegro."

"A lamb para mi father-in-law? No problema," Jim said. He laughed. "Hey, man, I'm really speaking muy bueno Spanish now. So where do I get a lamb?"

"I know where to buy a good one," Lalo said. The sombrero had tilted to one side, almost falling off his head. "Let's go right now. I can wake up a compadre of mine and we'll purchase a lamb from him, a young lamb with a smooth, white wool coat for good luck." As Lalo stood up, his hat fell to the floor.

Nacho left the bar to scoop up the hat. He handed it back to Lalo.

Pancho looked around the room and shook his head. He was happy that his friends were happy. He wanted a night to remember. But his compadres all looked so drunk none of them would remember a thing. Tomorrow they'll all be too busy curing their hangovers, he thought.

"Let's go get that lamb for mi suegro," Jim said. He started looking for the keys to his Lexus SUV. He fumbled around searching his pant pockets until he found them on the third search after much swearing.

"Nacho, you're our designated driver," Pancho said.

Pancho took off with Jim, Nacho and the compadre Lalo, who had rolled up his Mexican sombrero like a papyrus scroll and held it tucked under his arm.

◆

Nacho drove for several hours while his passengers slept. The sun was long up when Nacho pulled into Pancho's driveway. Marina, Pancho's wife, refused to open the front door when they knocked.

Pancho couldn't blame his wife for being angry since he'd been out all night drinking with his compadres. The four men and a small goat walked around the house to the back door.

"Why do you think you can come home after not even calling me last night?" Marina asked. Her voice was pretty loud and she looked very angry.

Pancho was concerned Jim would be scared away. "Come on in. Mi casa es tu casa. Come in. My wife Marina is a saint, as my compadre Lalo said. She is a good woman and raised such wonderful children."

"I think I'll take my goat and leave," Jim said.

"You can't do that," Pancho said. He was holding the rope that was tied around the goat's neck. "This goat represents your intention, your promise to support Sofía after you marry her. The goat stays with us."

Pancho was concerned Jim might elope with Sofía instead of marrying her the proper way in the cathedral but Marina's angry yelling interrupted his thoughts.

"You brought a damn goat instead of a lamb, as the tradition says?" She noticed the shaggy animal for the first time and rolled her eyes in disgust. "A goat is a bad omen," she said. "It has to be a lamb...."

"We couldn't find a lamb at 4 o'clock in the morning," Pancho said. He tried to diffuse Marina's temper. "We were lucky to get this kid goat at that hour. Don't worry, you can cook barbacoa with her. I'll bet it will taste great. Or roast the goat and make cabrito."

"So you were all drunk out of your skulls and you didn't even know what you got," Marina said. She looked at Jim. "If my daughter is to be your wife, then you have to follow our tradition and get a lamb. All my other daughters, all eight of them, received lambs."

Sofía came in the door. Pancho could tell Jim's heart melted when he saw her. He could tell this New York gringo loved Sofía. Pancho glanced at his daughter. She looked even more beautiful than usual. Her dark brown, shoulder length hair was curled at the tips instead of hanging straight. Pancho envisioned his daughter in a white wedding gown at the altar of St. Francis and figured he could not allow the young couple to consider eloping.

"What's all the commotion about a goat?" Sofía asked.

"The men are leaving to exchange this ratty looking goat for a lamb. You and I are going later today to St. Francis to ask Father Bartolomé to reserve a date for your wedding,"

Marina said. For the first time, she smiled. She glanced at her daughter and her smile became fuller and wider and even warm. Her eyes shined with love.

Pancho figured his wife was happy again. Her baby daughter was engaged. He knew Marina always enjoyed weddings, especially the ones involving her daughters.

"I know you don't understand all this nonsense about the goat, but if you want Sofía as your wife you'd better find a lamb to bring as a peace offering to Marina," Pancho said. "Let's go exchange this pinche trouble-making goat."

Pancho tied the goat in the hatchback of the SUV. As he knotted the rope he cursed under his breath. "There's a reason for the word 'cabron,'" he said.

Finally, with the goat tied down, all four men piled in and drove off with Nacho still acting as chauffeur.

◆

On the way back to Santa Fe, Jim held the lamb in his lap as Nacho drove. Pancho looked at Jim who was obviously suffering from a splitting headache. Pancho could tell that despite the hangover, Jim was not going to let anything happen to this cute little lamb. Pancho's eyes started watering. He needed to blow his nose. He searched his pockets for his red bandana handkerchief. When he couldn't find it, he used the back of his hand to wipe the snot.

"As angry as Marina seemed over the goat being a bad omen, we'd better not tell her it strangled itself in the rear of the vehicle," Nacho said, breaking the silence in the SUV. He looked at Jim. "She'd really consider that bad luck. We ought to stop and wash this vehicle and drive by St. Francis for a bottle of holy water to sprinkle over all the seats and the rear where the goat died to get rid of la mala suerte."

"To get rid of bad luck, I guess we should have buried

the goat," Jim said. "I had to pay for the stupid goat anyway."

"Pues, I think my compadre would not waste a good goat that got tangled up in a rope and accidentally hanged itself," Lalo said. The old man had his sombrero back on his head. "I'll bet the compadre is stoking a fire in the barbecue pit right now. I think I'll go back and visit him tonight. He makes the best barbacoa."

Pancho and Nacho agreed with Lalo about the compadre's barbacoa. As Nacho parked the SUV in front of St. Francis, Pancho saw Sofía and his wife standing next to the priest outside the cathedral. Then he saw Sofía running down the steps towards the vehicle. Marina and the priest, a few paces behind Sofía, were heading towards the SUV, too.

"Jim, get out of the car. Hurry. We'll drive away and wash the car," Pancho said.

Pancho knew he had to keep the women from getting in the SUV if he was going to save an engagement. Marina could not find out about the goat strangling itself. "Hurry up before they get here."

Jim barely got onto the sidewalk when Nacho drove off fast, so fast he burned rubber. Jim was still holding the lamb.

"Mira que lindo," Marina said. She turned to Sofía and said. "Now this beautiful little creature is a good omen."

"She's perfect," Sofía said. She hugged Jim and kissed the little lamb in his arms.

"Why don't we all go into the church to bless the lamb? I'll sprinkle a little holy water over the little creature," Father Bartolomé said. "Just for good luck."

The two women and Jim followed the priest into the cathedral.

◆

Jim, Sofía and Marina stood next to Pancho's bed at the hospital. Pancho opened his eyes, rolling his eyeballs around, surveying the room.

"How in pinche hell did I get here?" he asked.

"You should have died in that accident, you old fool," Marina said. "You were so drunk you just rolled around in the SUV."

"What are you talking about, woman?" Pancho asked.

"You and Lalo had an accident in my SUV," Jim said. "The two of you returned to the goat compadre's house instead of washing my vehicle."

Marina was furious. She paced the room. Sofía's eyes followed her mother's pacing.

"Oh, yeah, the barbecue was delicious." Pancho said. He closed his eyes and licked his lips. When he opened his eyes again, they were bright and sparkling. "Man, I tell you, the compadre makes the best goat barbacoa."

"Pendejo," Marina said. She stopped pacing and stood by Pancho's bed again. "You wrecked Jim's Lexus. Worse yet, you tied that goat so tight in the vehicle that it choked itself. Then you went back last night with Lalo and ate that poor little goat. I cannot believe you're such an irresponsible, insensitive pendejo. That poor little animal...."

"Lalo? Was Lalo in the accident, too?" Pancho asked.

"Of course he was. He's as irresponsible as you," Marina said. "The two of you were brought to the hospital in an ambulance."

"So where is my compadre Nacho?"

"He was the only sane one. You dropped him off at his Cantina because he had to open it again. So he wasn't with you two pendejos," Marina said. "If Nacho had been with you two idiots, none of this would have happened."

Sofía put her arms around her mother and hugged her. "Let it be, mamacita. Don't get so upset. It's not good for you."

"Upset? Upset? Living with this pendejo, that's the way my life is. I'm always upset. He upsets me all the time. Look at him. Broken bones, bruises and he's savoring the barbacoa from last night. From that poor little goat...."

"Please, Marina, calm down before you have a heart attack. It's not worth it," Jim said. He placed his hand on Marina's shoulder. "I have insurance. The vehicle will get fixed. Pancho and Lalo both survived. We have lots to be thankful for."

"Thankful for this idiot always ruining things?" Marina asked. "You and Sofía have my blessing to elope. We don't need this idiot messing up your wedding."

◆

Sofía looked splendid in her wedding dress with the long tail. The photographer was taking photos of the bride and groom outside St. Francis cathedral. The newlyweds looked joyful.

"Let's get a photo of the whole family," Jim said. He kissed the bride as the photographer snapped a few more shots.

"Really, the whole family?" Sofía asked. She looked skeptical. "That would be 279 people. Don't you know how big my family is?"

"Okay, never mind. I forgot the family was that big," Jim said. "Let's finish up here and move on to the reception."

In the stretch limo, Marina beamed. Pancho, his arm in a sling, sat next to his wife. He was quiet and content.

"I have to be on good behavior," Pancho said. "That's what my lovely wife has told me."

The bride and groom sat holding hands in the rear of the limo looking into each other's eyes. When the entourage arrived at the reception hall, Jim climbed out of the limo first. He helped Marina out. As he did, he whispered to his mother-in-law.

"Pancho has been peaceful and quiet for days. What's going on?"

Marina looked behind her and made sure her husband and Sofía were still in the limo. "Don't tell anyone, but I'm giving him toloache in his coffee every morning to keep him calm."

"Tolo what?" Jim asked.

"It's an old Mexican herbal remedy," Marina whispered.

"You're putting what into Pancho's coffee?" Jim asked. "You mean without his knowledge?"

"You and Sofía enjoy your honeymoon," Marina said. "We can talk about it when you return."

Sofía was ready to join her bridegroom. Jim reached out to help his bride. She smiled like a princess as she stepped out of the limo.

Bob Lindsey

An Old Woman

(for Goldie)

The old woman sits
like a silence wind,

her eyes singing to
salt, gray waters

rolling ashore

thoughts of almost
bare trees and

leaves that hang on
in November

her lips lie waiting for words,
hungry for flowers to bloom

once again.

At the Bait House

Tires crunch
on the oyster shell road
telling me
another fisherman is
bringing his boat
to launch dockside,
a magnificent
specimen,
long, sleek with a motor
the size of a tree trunk
gets a mile
to the gallon
two fishing buddies
jump from a king cab
guide the boat
'til it floats clear
of the long trailer
sunscreen, bait,
ice, poles,
anticipation
all loaded on
board
off with a roar
on the rocking
waters,
their mutilated laughter
swallowed by the sea
back later with their catch

held high
like a string of pearls
for all to see.

Barbara Williams Lewis

Stone Mother

There is a mask in Janie's garden.
A symbol of fertility.
She sits stone-faced
At the edge of the pavilion.
Her back is to the water.
She is surrounded by lilies:
Plantains, tigers, I think,
And lovely tall grasses.

Her back is to the horizon on purpose.
She draws in the power of the water
To nurture Janie's garden.
She absorbs the energy
To share with her sisters.
She attracts those
Who would pass her.
With a blind eye
She makes them see.

Without softness
She is tender.
Without light
She brings joy.
She has no hair, no teeth,
Yet she is complete.
She has learned to be
Bigger than trauma.

If you bring your troubles to her
She utters no sound.
She, alas, speaks to your soul
In ways no other has done.

I call her Stone Mother.
Perhaps I should call her Mother Stone.
She told me that I cannot fix what is broken
If I continue to use the tools that broke it.

Stone Mother. Mother Stone.
Jasper, Hematite, Unakite, Jade,
Obsidian, Pearl, Ruby, Diamond.
These are her sisters.
Like the daughters of Zeus and Mnemosyne
They all have healing powers.
It is Mother Stone, however,
The Stone Mother
Who gives them directive.

Workshop in Photos

Photos by
Pamela Booton / Sophie Rousmaniere / Kathryn Lane

SHERROD
VILLAGE

Jay Minton

The Bell

Prosaic is the party
that no one has attended.
How surely can it be
That the host was quite offended.
"Where could they be!"
he yelled aloud
his ego being less than proud.
"I think I'll call them on the phone."
He rang them all,
not one was home.
"They must be on their way, I see."
He waited up till half past three
and as he wandered off to bed
such excuses filled his head.
"I must have given wrong direction
or all came down with staff infection.
Maybe there was a traffic jam?
Or they must have stopped to fix a dam.
Nevertheless no one has shown
my Friday night has just been blown."
And as he tucked himself to sleep
on his porch a soul did creep.
The doorbell rang—
the host's heart jumped.
"It's them after all,
I've not been dumped!"
He ran quite swiftly to the door.

Oh the fun that was in store:
the moment rising
the door gave a creak
followed by the crickets cheep.
No one was there.
He stood and stared.
"God damn ding dong ditching!"
he declared.
"How I hate that awful game."
He went back to sleep
All hope was slain.

Aubrey Parker

Circles

In life, we all travel in circles. The size of the circle depends upon the stage of our life.

As a child our circles are small: School, Church, grandmother's house, and home.

In our teens our circles venture further as we test our wings. Sometimes one may go too far to find a learning experience.

In our professional lives the circumference of the circle expands and may cross state lines or continents. These circles depend upon our level of ambition, training, confidence and education.

During our declining years our circles shrink to smaller and smaller orbits until our circles become a rectangle two feet by six feet and we find peace.

Stupor

Scraps of drunken paper
Litter the floor
In the Id sanctum of hidden thoughts
Proof of madness or brain rot

In the light of day
Scraps of drunken paper
Often lose the thought
Illegible penmanship whatever wrote

Days and years may pass
And in time reviewed
Understanding finally found
Leaving one confused

Have aliens abducted me?
And pushed the pen
For all to see
Or is this me?

The Silver Clasp

In every heart deep inside
Lies a silver clasp
Hidden from prying eyes.
It shines with memories
Tried and true
Unsnapped and opened
Sometimes to view.
Silver memories
In a gossamer haze
Gazed through glistening tears
Of yesterdays
As time speeds tenfold
$E=MC^2$ now reveals
Slow motion life.
One now reviews
Memories kept at the back of book
Surface again as one begins to look
And see one's mistakes.
To repair now is much too late
So in silent prayer past midnight hour
Contrite recompense
Cannot relive again
So close the clasp
And sleep again.

Kindergarten

Things I learned in Kindergarten. My parents put me in Kindergarten when I was four years old. If my mother had not taught me to read when I was three it certainly would have been more brutal than it was. The rest of the children were six or seven and had a real head start of me in cognitive ability, size, and criminal traits.

Distrust:

My first lesson, some of the boys had a little wooden toy that was a box that had a sliding top. When the top was opened a little snake with a nail for a tooth came out of it. So they were putting gumdrops on the nail and when one of their friends would open the box, the reward would be a piece of candy. But every time I would open the box the nail would stick me. Hmmm...maybe that is where the saying getting nailed came from.

Flavors:

All crayons taste the same.

Paste:

Only the firm paste is edible, the runny stuff tastes bad.

My Left Thumb

My left thumb has had a hard life. It has been attacked on multiple occasions by the right hand. It often seems that the right hand has a mission of destroying the archrival on the left.

A multitude of weapons has been used, from claw hammers, ball-peen hammers, torches, gasoline and matches.

Several years ago (as an act of mercy, I suppose), all feeling in the thumb was lost because the right hand severed the nerve bundle for the thumb and his two adjacent fingers. The weapon of choice was a machete to the wrist under the thinly veiled guise of swatting a wasp.

Most recently while working on a metal sculpture with a 2000-degree welding torch, the right hand assaulted the left thumb thereby burning the poor thumb to the bone.

My left thumb is not happy. It cries all night long.

Newton's Third Law

For every force and action there is an equal force and reaction. This theory applies to much more than physics.

As a young man, losing my father to the sea was a force to cause reaction in my life. I found myself suddenly imbued with his character traits, which had often been detested before. He was a kind man with deep compassion and understanding. After all, he did put up with my rebellious youth. So my everyday life and decisions were rebooted and I started thinking of others before myself instead of being an asshole.

It is my tenet and credo to never lose a friend.

The Gift

On a cold dreary day
With nothing to do
I found my box of comforts
And keepsakes true

Wedding rings
Those have lost their glow
Children's gifts
Of love to grow

But one of my favorites
A simple handmade box
Tattered and torn
But still very warm

Forever ago your hands
Folded together
A small gift
Of friendship true

In life's calm persistence
Dreams drift away
But simple gifts
Shine always

Now I hear footsteps
Father Time runs away
And the haywain creaks nearer
Day by day

Sophie Rousmaniere

SONGKRAN

Damn, the sun was hot that morning. The blaring sun beaded on my brow as I fired up my motorcycle and zoomed off into the chaos of the day.

Little more than half way down the street came the first icy blasts of water, next came the buckets, I was waterlogged by the time I reached the first stoplight. Traffic was horrendous, it took 15 minutes to go 100 meters through the gridlocked masses of pick up trucks, masses of pedestrians and the constant deluge of cold murky water.

This is Songkran, Thailand's most honored and thoroughly celebrated holiday, where the whole town dons all kinds of waterpower from tiny squirt guns to buckets to high power hoses for four days of insanity in celebration of the new year. The idea is to wash away the sins of the year, to cleanse and to renew. The word Songkan is originally derived from a Sanskrit word meaning the beginning of the solar year, the passage into a new sign of the zodiac. In Thai the word means beginning, or change.

The origin of the celebration goes back to a fertility ceremony for the pre-Buddhist Dai people of northern Vietnam. The Tai people that migrated from Southern China, whose blood runs in the veins of many present day Thais, also had a water festival. The festival was in commemoration of rice harvest, but was celebrated during the first lunar month; many say that this is the way that Songkran came to Northern Thailand. Buddhist and Brahman beliefs migrated here from Northern India and Sri Lanka. Water festivals there brought the religious element to the party. Chiang Mai is known as the best place to play in the water. According to the Bangkok Post, last year Songkran drew 134,225 tourists, both Thai and foreigners. As the party approaches, many businesses close, people spend their days drunk in the streets, playing with water or sitting casually talking with friends and visiting family.

Thais celebrate three New Year's parties—31 of December, Chinese New Year in February, and April 13, Songkran. April is the hottest month of the year, traditionally the event took place when the sun passes out of the zodiac sign of Pisces, now the day has solidified at the13th of April. At this time the mythical serpent-dragon Naga spouts ephemeral waters from his lair in the Mekhong River, the more water he spouts, the more rain will come. The rainy season also starts at this time. It is a time for young girls and boys to meet: in history a boy might offer a young girl a bowl of rice in representation of survival.

Many people also leave the city to visit their families, to regather and celebrate their kinship. In the countryside water play can last up to two weeks. The elderly are honored in a ceremony where the young ask for forgiveness for the sins of the past year, the youth pour scented water from silver bowls onto the hands of the elderly, while the young offer blessings of long life and happiness to come. A white powdery paste is smeared on people's faces to ward off evil, and to scare away bad spirits, now this tradition has developed into bright blue and red colors, running down the neck and onto clothes, this colorful pastime adds spice to the party. In the midst of water mania someone might approach another with outstretched hands,with string to tie on another's wrist. With three knots the person would traditionally utter blessings of good will as they tie the knots, these are not to be taken off, to be left until they fall off on their own. Some people may end up with 20 strings attached, this would be a great sign of respect and wholesome good will from others.

Colorfully clad in traditional dress, native "Hill Tribe" ladies walk the streets vending a variety of thin bracelets weaved from grass, along with small home woven bags. Locals flock to nearby temples to add wooden supports to old revered bodhi trees, in hopes of making merit for good luck in the coming year. All the temples cleanse the Buddha therein, with scented water.

Among the masses thronging at the most prominent wat, Wat Phra Singh, a line of people waited around the central Buddha image where one by one people bring incense, candles, and flower scented water to make merit, ask the Buddha for good luck and pour a cup of the liquid over the image after praying with hands in a prayer position, lighting incense and candles. As we stood in the blinding sunlight glinting off the golden image, a few policemen got into an argument. One older officer, obviously drunk was being involuntarily chaperoned away from the crowds--the scene got messy when he was not prepared to leave, ending up on the hot pavement, flailing and slobbering, he bit one of the domineering cop's kneecaps and soon got a few swift kicks.

A few people apologized to us for having to see such a sight; we laughed it off and assured them it was just as amusing to us as it was to the rest of the stunned and snickering crowd. So back into the slippery mess we charged, racing through the streets in the blinding sun, turning away to avoid the heavy deluge of flying water, we laughed until we were glowing.

People leap into the city's filthy canals, swimming in such waters is known to be somewhat dangerous, but the drenched masses don't seem to care, even in Bangkok, where the water may contain various dangerous diseases.

Many spend their days drunk in the streets, partying with friends and blowing off the pressurized steam of the last year. Thai people in general are somewhat subdued.

Motor scooters are the preferred mode of transport in Chiang Mai; when the water starts, traveling can be very dangerous. Pickup trucks loaded with liquid artillery fill the streets, where getting across town could take hours in the heavy traffic. Ice water, canal water, river water, scented water, all water is plentiful. It is a thrill when a lone dry person walks by, some try to plead mercy, but none is given. Monks and police are fair game as well, although the water for them is a bit more respectfully shed. In Ban Cradi, outside of Bangkok, the Mon people celebrate old tradition without the ruckus of the outside world. Here there is a tradition in which monks bathe themselves in the privacy of temple quarters, then change back into dry robes for the blessing of the people. All household Buddha images are cleansed with scented water, a variety of herbs are burned and dropped into the water along with fresh and dry flowers. Water balloons are hurtled through through train windows, accidents abound and people do get hurt. According to the Bangkok post, in the three days leading up to Songkran 472 people were killed in motor accidents, 844 injured. Most accidents were due to drunk and reckless driving, despite the 1,800 extra highway police deployed. Drug traffickers use the influx of motor travel to transport their contraband amongst the masses of vehicles. “Songkran is a time for visiting relatives and family; before Songkran was not aggressive, everyone called out to each other on the streets.

People did not use expensive water pistols, it is now becoming a fashion and a buisness. People get expensive water pistols to look cool, others sell them to make money” said Pow, of Chiang Mai.

The four days of Songkran go as follows: The first two days are called the “Troot Festival,” these are the last days of the old year, the word means endings and beginnings. Festivities start as early as the eleventh, with drumming and gong competitions, many districts are represented, each group coming from a different temple to show their skills. Traditional “Lanna” performances of dance and culture are also performed. “Lanna” in direct translation means one million rice fields, it is referred to as a time in history in Northern Thailand, when the culture was not tainted by “farang” (western people) influence. This was a time in history before factories replaced rice fields, and the people lived off the land in the old ways.

Musical performances accompanying theatrical shows, where traditional instruments are played accompanying the famous Thai fingernail dance, are demonstrated, with skits depicting life in the olden days. The first official day of Troot (called "wan sungkharn Lohng") begins with people dressing in traditional clothes, and cleansing their homes in lieu of the coming new year, there are demonstrations of traditional dance, and the first parade takes place. Each district of Chiang Mai province is represented in the procession that crosses the city by the main thoroughfare, beauty queens with parasols to guard them from water and sun walk along one of the city's major streets towards the most revered temple in Chiang Mai, Wat Pha Singh. Some of the lovely ladies walk stoically, or dance as they go, others grin wet smiles from the tops of brilliantly decorated floats. The clanging of gongs resonate throughout the city.

Buddha images from each temple are paraded through the streets and showered by the masses atop flowered floats for cleansing. At night, the same street is transformed into a massive buffet of local specialties offered by many of the city's restaurants. The wafting scents of spicy curries and frying grease fill the air, tables covered in colorful sweets entice the senses with a huge variety of brightly colored mushy, juicy, chewy, sweet delights. Traditional music is blasted out to the crowd from a small stage as the masses gorge themselves.

"Wan Nao" is the day in between years, people gather buckets of soft river sand from the banks of the Ping River. The next day, they will bring the sand to the city's temples to replace that which has left on the soles of the feet of the many visitors that year. Musical events go on at various cultural centers, children's beauty contests parade by, alongside a bicycle powered pageant where the lovely ladies are delicately perched atop mechanical beauties.

The first day of the new year is called "Wan payawan". The morning is greeted by throngs of people bringing fruit, foodstuffs and prepared dishes and new orange robes to monks at a local temple. Together, families sit before a bald, orange-robed monk where each member's wrist is tied together by a white symbolic rope to encourage protection and unity in the family, the blessing intended for this existence and in the afterlife. He blesses the people with prayers and a light showering of holy water. This is the day, traditionally when the water play began; these days, however, the streets have already been thoroughly soaked. Although the water had been shed for many days this year, the rule is that on Wan Payawan, 12:00 noon is the time when water play is allowed to begin (of course this rule is not so wholeheartedly observed). In the past water was gently poured over the back of one's shoulder with a smile, now the water play can get near violent.

At home, silver bowls pour flowery water on the hands of the elderly in respect and good will. The sand gathered the day before is erected into small chedis (a conical temple structure, also known as a pagoda). These are presented in many styles and decorated intricately, after hours of preparation, the temples are ready for the judging of the finest specimen.

On a small stage at a Buddhist school awards are given for the finest pagoda, accompanied by light melodic music, the trophies are presented by a traditionally adorned beauty queen and an announcer with a loud microphone. A traditional drumming contest is held at the cultural center, and much festivies of the slobbering drunk linger on into the night.

April 15 is the day when all family and religious affairs are finished and everyone can just relax and have fun. There always seems to be a parade going on down that same thoughoughfare, with more bright costumes and clanging gongs than you can count. For the next few days the whole town has a hangover, many restaurants that stayed open for the party now close, everyone takes some time to recuperate, the streets are quiet again, whirring softly with the stirring of average daily life in Chiang Mai.

Already plans for next year's party are in effect—in perpetual anticipation of Chiang Mai's greatest annual party——Songkran.

Thai Magic Tattoos: More than Skin Deep

Small groups of men and boys crowded around a temple doorway in the misty dawn of morning. Inside, forty shirtless sat on mats on the floor, focusing their attention on the work of two Thai monks with long pointed rods, carefully inscribing magical amulets on the backs of two men. The room was alive with giddy, yet respectful anticipation. Each of the onlookers patiently waited for his turn to be tattooed. The monks mumbled magical Buddhist scripture verses as they methodically tapped the design into the skin.

This was just the beginning of the annual Wai Kru festival at Wat Bang Phra temple in Nakon Pratom Province in central Thailand. The Huge Temple is famous for its tattooing monks and the power they breathe into their designs. Wai Kru translates to 'honor the teacher', and it is here that the power of Thai magic tattoos can be witnessed first hand on a large scale. Pilgrims from all over Thailand and the world converge for one morning every spring to take part in the largest festival of 'magic' tattoos in the world.

'Sak Yan', or magic tattoos have Buddhist, spiritual and 'voodoo-like' implications. In Thailand, Burma, Laos and Cambodia it is believed that these tattoos, empowered by verse, meditation and ritual have the potential to ward off evil, protect against bullets, knives, snakes, ghosts, and any number of other dangers. 'Pali' script (pronounced 'baa-lee') is a derivative of Sanskrit amd is the language of Buddhist scriptures in this area. It can be formulated into spells and blessings, as well as used for magical and protective purposes in a 'supernatural' capacity. It is this text, sometimes accompanied by pictures of animals, humans and geometric designs that, tattooed into the skin, contain a an amazing power.

For centuries Thai military and police have worn magic tattoos for protection. In ancient wars it was the only protective armor worn in battle. These are still the most common variety. There are designs concerned with dharma, the Buddha's teachings, which bring the wearer 'Buddha power' to calm and focus the mind. Designs like the tiger, snake, rooster, elephant, pig, Hanuman, and others each contain their own distinct powers.

By 7:00am the colorful altar was overflowing with tasty looking offerings, photos of important monks, statues of the Buddha, fruits and flowers. Under tall golden tiered umbrellas two adorned pig heads blankly stared into space, wafting cumulonimbus clouds of incense smoke. All of this was overshadowed by a huge image of the temple's highest revered and recently departed teacher Lang Poor Perm. The main field, about half an acre wide, was sectioned off by holy ropes. It was filling up fast with devotees who took their seats facing the stage as the sun rose above the horizon.

After some time, fierce screams and screeching yells began to resound from the audience. First, it was the trumpeting of an elephant, then the roar of a tiger. People panted heavily and contorted their faces into unnatural expressions as they one by one jumped up and charged toward the large altar/stage with wild, entranced eyes. With invisible claws bared they ran and threw themselves at the huge altar with a fury. Snakes and crocodiles slithered, hissing on their bellies through muddy gravel, while Hanuman, the monkey god, screeched hysterically as he danced. Roosters clucked and crowed as they came, birds soared with wings spread.

Civilian guards stood guarding the altar, ready to grab the crazed runners as they approached. The guards snatched them off their feet, one by one. It took three or more to secure one of the screaming, writhing bodies. They released each delusional devotee by lifting the moaning, kicking, squealing person off the ground and tugging forcefully at their earlobe. When awakened from the trance, each walked solemnly back to their seat on the ground and waited for the next time they might be driven into trance.

Like freight trains, they trampled all people in their paths, the echoing cries becoming more and more frequent as time progressed. The announcement over the loud speaker said that at exactly 9:00am the whole place was going to go nuts. The stampede began instantaneously. Writhing masses of bodies all sweating and panting in the collective heat mashed together in a massive simultaneous charge. Cheers and exclamations, muffled voices jabbered all at once, as holy water sprayed out from huge hoses mounted on the stage, as monks doused the elated mass of human bodies with holy water mist....

Tattoos have different meanings and origins all around the world. While some may get them for aesthetic reasons, others have deep meaning to the wearer. Tattoos have significant spiritual meanings throughout traditional and tribal communities and around the world, whether denoting status, belonging or individuality. As tattoos become more socially acceptable in modern times, those of us who choose to adorn ourselves may also be somehow trying to connect to some ancient power or tribal tradition we may not find in our Western lives. Here tattoos aren't merely tribal or creative; they are taken very seriously as a spiritual practice and a means by which to connect with a higher power.

Hazel Ward

Whimsy

I am planted here in this garden
of perfect fits...
lush sweet potato vines flow around me
green carpet pillows for the humble bee.
Purple wisteria float and float
to where I cannot see...
My neighbors' world in dappled light.

All are fragrant,
brilliant colored hues
I am not.

What am I?

A pumpkin yellow pig stuck to the ground.
Body rotund.
A snout that will never learn to root...
Too tiny and Rubenesque.
I am the indecorous decoration
discreet and still.

Why cast me, a misfit,
at the curved edge?

An iridescent butterfly hovers,
spying my red tipped wings
drops down, down
hovers uncertainly

then sharply flies away...

I resemble no butterfly,
graceless, pushed low to the ground,
unspread wings that cannot fly.
Pigs would not own me either...
What pig has blue ears, stuck too high?
I can neither slide nor glide,
nor fly...
Can perform no feat of daring,
only sit and mark a spot.
My place in a garden ill defined
Incongrous, but yet it's mine!

Lowell Mick White

After the Sad Garage Sale I Made a Decision

It got hot sometimes where I lived then, on the edge of the plains, dry and hot, and the wind blowing all the time, and on those days it was good to have air conditioning. Even if it was just a window unit, it was good to have, and I could sit inside—our home—and be cool with Molly and the dogs. Everything, I thought, was fine. But all of a sudden I didn't have air conditioning any more—I didn't have Molly, or the dogs, and I didn't even have electricity, and I was left with nothing to do but sit back in the recliner, drink a cold beer from an ice chest, smoke a cigarette, and think about things. Think about—brood about, ponder about, cogitate about, wonder about—whatever the hell had just happened.

And that's when the air conditioner started to move.

It made a grinding sound, waggling up and down in the window. I looked at it for a moment, then got up out of the chair and went out on the front steps.

My neighbor—my friend, too, I guess he was my friend—Joe Sullivan, was standing there with his hands on the air conditioner.

"Oh, hey there," Sullivan said. "I thought you left."

He didn't look startled or even embarrassed, trying to run off with my air conditioner.

"The lease here—" I said. Was canceled. It was hard to explain. I said, "I'm still around."

I sort of lifted my left hand for a beer, then realized that I'd left the beer—and the cigarette, too—sitting on the table next to the chair.

"Tell you what," Sullivan said. He was leaning on the air conditioner, squinting in the sunlight, crinkling his eyes at me. "I'll give you twenty-five bucks for it."

"What?"

"Twenty-five bucks for the air conditioner."

I blinked, squinted back at him, squinted past him at the street, the other houses, the hot pale late summer sky. Then I squinted back at him some more.

"Are you crazy? I just bought that new last May. It's only—" I stopped and tried to count. It was September, but I couldn't remember offhand how many months that was from May—five six, four, it seemed forever. "It's only a summer old."

"It's not running," he said. "It's busted."

"That's because the electric's turned off," I said.

Molly didn't pay the bill or something.

Molly didn't do a lot of things. But maybe she did.

"Okay, then," Sullivan said. "Fifty dollars."

"Maybe I'll need AC at my new place," I said. "Forget it."

I went back in the house and saw that the cigarette had rolled out of the ashtray somehow and was burning a hole in the filthy carpet, smoldering. I picked it up and poured some beer on the blackened burn spot and settled back into my chair and started staring some more at the wall. That's all I pretty much wanted to do. Then I heard a little tapping noise and looked up and saw Sullivan standing in the doorway.

"Can I come in?"

He came in before I could tell him No.

I said, "The air conditioner's not for sale."

"No," he said, "I just wanted to see how you were doing."

I shrugged and he walked on over and sat on the couch. The couch was in tatters, chewed to pieces by the dogs when Molly left them locked up in the house for two weeks while she was off with her boyfriend smoking crack or whatever she was doing.

Those poor damn dogs!

Locked up like that—no food, no water. Just a couch to chew on.

I thought Molly loved those dogs.

I looked at Sullivan, that poor damn couch all torn apart.

He was lucky a spring didn't screw him in the ass.

"That's a nice TV," Sullivan said. "Sony."

"It's not for sale, either," I said. The TV was mounted high enough on the wall that the dogs couldn't get to it.

"No, I was just thinking it was a nice TV." Sullivan took off his cap and ran his hand across his head, then put the cap back on. "Too bad you don't have electricity. We could watch the Chiefs."

Oh, I thought. Football. This must be Sunday.

Tomorrow's Monday, then.

Well, shit.

I looked over at Sullivan. He wasn't a bad guy, he was a neighbor, he was sort of a friend, he only wanted a cheap air conditioner.

"Want a beer?" I asked. I gestured at the blue plastic cooler next to the chair. "I stocked up."

"Sure." He got up and pulled a can out of the cooler and settled back onto the couch. He had only just sat down and already couch stuffing was sticking to his clothes.

"You talked to Molly?" he asked.

"Not since she left." Why would I want to talk to a crazy woman?

Sullivan shook his head and popped open the can of beer and took a long drink.

"The beer's cold," he said.

"I bought some ice, too," I said.

"Yeah," Sullivan said. "You know, I think Molly went

kind of crazy while you were gone."

I nodded at that. "Yeah, I guess."

"Yeah," Sullivan said. "She went through some sort of manic phase."

Sullivan and his wife had dozens—maybe hundreds—of self-help books in their house. I was over there once and I stood staring at those shelves of books, shocked, wondering what they were good for. But apparently they were good for something, though, because Sullivan and his wife were still together and Molly and I weren't, and his wife was sane and Molly wasn't, and he had electricity and I didn't, and my house was all torn to shreds and his wasn't.

And also, yeah, Molly went fucking crazy or something.

There was a tap at the door and we looked up. The old lady from next door was standing there. Mrs. Borgan. She was a little old lady whose husband was retired from the post office.

"Hello, there!" she said. She sounded very cheerful, she was always very cheerful, and she looked at me and smiled. "I just came to see how you were doing."

"He's doing fine," Sullivan said. "He's really hanging in there."

I glanced sideways at Sullivan and sat up and pulled another beer from the cooler.

"Care for a beer?" I asked Mrs. Borgan.

"Oh, no, thank you," she said. She came on into the house and looked around. "Oh, my."

I sat back in the chair. Yeah. Oh fucking my. That's pretty much what our landlord had said, too, when he saw the place. I had only been back a day, not even a day, and was trying to figure out what the deal was with Molly—she was there when I got back, wild, and she drove away and drove back again, wilder, and the dogs were jumping around half-starved and crazed—when the landlord stopped by for an inspection. Someone, I guess, had tipped him off about the dogs. He took one look and said, "Oh, my" and then he told us to get the hell out. Molly said "Fine" and threw a few things together and gathered the dogs and got in her car and drove away. I hadn't seen her since.

"I didn't know things were this bad," Mrs. Borgan said. She wandered off into the kitchen, stepping carefully to avoid the piles of dog shit on the carpet.

I looked over at Sullivan and he shrugged.

"The Chiefs kind of suck again this year," he said after a moment.

I thought about that for a long minute. Then I nodded and said, "Yeah."

We heard a noise in the kitchen and then Mrs. Borgan came through, pushing the microwave oven on a little cart.

"Molly said I could have this," she said. "Something to remember her by."

"She wanted you to have the microwave?"

"Uh-huh." Mrs. Borgan gave a little grunt as she pushed the cart from the kitchen linoleum up onto the carpet. The little wheels of the cart crushed a dog turd into the carpet but Mrs. Borgan didn't notice.

"Jesus," I said. "Why don't you just take a plant or something?" We had lots of plants around the house. They were all looking pretty sickly and battered since whatever had happened to Molly had happened.

"Why, thank you, Dan," she said cheerfully. She unhooked a big fern from a ceiling hook over by the blank television set and placed it unsteadily on top of the microwave.

I got up out of the chair.

"Listen, I can't let you take the oven," I said.

"Why not? Molly said I could have it."

I thought about that. I asked, "Have you talked to her recently?"

"No, but she *always* said I could have her oven

if something happened to her. She always loved my microwave roasted chicken, and this oven's so much better than mine—" she patted the oven "—and she said that if anything happened to her, she'd feel better knowing I had her oven. Every time I roast a chicken in it I'll think of her."

"I don't know for sure if anything happened to Molly," I said. "I haven't talked to her."

"She went crazy," Mrs. Borgan said. "Everybody says so."

Everybody said so.

"I'll have to talk to Molly first," I said. "When I do I'll ask her about the oven."

Mrs. Borgan stood there looking disappointed, sticking her lower lip out, pouting. She looked like a wrinkly little girl.

"You can keep the plant," I said. I picked it up and handed it to her.

She looked at it doubtfully. She said, "It's kind of sick,"

"I'm sure you can fix it." I looked around for something else to give her. I spotted a deer skull on the mantle over the fireplace. It had one antler—the left one—and had been bleached white by the sun. Molly and I had found it while hiking once in Big Bend National Park. I know there's some law against taking artifacts from national parks, but we took it anyway. I had always felt kind of guilty about having it. But now I reached over and took the skull off the mantle and handed it to her. Passing on the guilt.

"Molly would want you to have this," I said.

Mrs. Borgan looked at the skull closely, holding it by the antler. "Donnie might like it," she said. Donnie was her grandson.

"Molly always did like Donnie," I said. I guessed, I didn't know—who the hell knew what Molly liked or didn't like? I didn't.

I pulled another beer from the blue cooler and sank

back into my chair. I glanced over at Sullivan. He was sitting quietly on the ruined couch, sipping his beer. I realized I'd have to give him something, too, now. But I'd be damned if I was going to give him my air conditioner. Not even for twenty-five dollars.

Mrs. Borgan stood holding the skull and the fern, looking around the room.

"It's so odd she left and didn't take her things. I watched her leave—she just threw her bag in the car and put those three big dogs in the back seat and off she drove."

"Yeah." I said. I hadn't really tried to stop her, either. Actually, by that time I was kind of scared of her. What can you do with a determined crazy woman? The landlord and I stood on the steps and watched her drive away. Molly drove down the street, made a U-turn, and came back. I thought maybe she'd come to her senses or something but all she did was get out of the car and take down a hummingbird feeder that was hanging from the sycamore. The dogs sat in the back of the car watching her. "I forgot this," she said, and then she got back in the car and drove off, and this time she didn't come back. I went back in the house and shut the door, leaving the landlord on the steps. I'd only gotten home from Atlanta the night before everything happened, and I'd been awake pretty much since then and I was tired then and I was still tired and Molly was off stealing cars and robbing banks and being a terrorist or whatever all she'd been doing—doing whatever it was a determined crazy woman did.

"She didn't take much clothing with her, did she?" Mrs. Borgan asked.

"No." I knew what she was getting at but I suddenly didn't care. "No, she only took a few things."

"Hmm." Mrs. Borgan sat the fern and the skull down and wandered off towards the bedroom.

"Microwave roasted chicken," Sullivan said. "How can

it get brown and crispy in a microwave?"

"Fuck if I know," I said.

"Yeah," Sullivan said. After a moment he said, "I like my chicken skin crispy."

We sat there in the hot, dim room. I could hear the old lady moving stuff around in the bedroom.

"Have you ever taken a personality test?" Sullivan asked.

"No," I said. I looked at him. Squinted, even though we were inside. "*What*?"

"A personality test," Sullivan said. He reached over and got another can of beer out of the cooler and opened it. "They have these tests where they figure out what your personality style is." He took a long drink of beer. "We use those at work so we can work better as a team."

"I'm not on a team."

"Me," Sullivan said, "I'm an extravert. I figure you for an introvert. I don't know about Molly, though—I never could figure her out. But I bet if you guys took one of those tests you could figure out how your personalities all fit together."

"Right now I'm not real interested in how our personalities fit together."

"That's because you're in mourning," Sullivan said, nodding. "You're experiencing deep grief. That's to be expected at this stage."

Mrs. Borgan came out of the bedroom with an armload of Molly's clothes—blouses, shorts, a couple of her nice work suits.

"These all need to be laundered," she said. "They all sort of smell like dog stuff. You know? I told Molly I'd look after her things if something happened to her." She headed for the door.

"Don't forget your skull," I said.

"I'll be back!" she called from the porch.

"I've got some books you should read," Sullivan said.

"They're all about relationships."

"I'm not in a relationship," I said. I stared at the blank TV. There was a big spot of light reflected from the open door.

Then the spot of light went dim and there was a knock on the doorframe. I looked up and Alma Garcia was there. She lived next door to old Mrs. Borgan, and her husband worked for the same federal agency I did. She smiled and waved at me through the screen and came on in.

"I heard you guys are having a sale."

"Not really."

Alma looked around. "Wow, it really is bad in here, huh?"

"You should've seen it before," Sullivan said. "Dan's really been working on getting things straightened up."

I guess he was trying to help me out, make it seem like I was taking control or whatever.

"I heard you left Molly and she went crazy," Alma said. "Billy says he hasn't seen you at work for a while."

"They sent me to Atlanta to work on a task force for a couple weeks" I said.

"Ah," she said, as if that explained everything. "I'm glad Billy doesn't have to travel. I might go crazy, too."

"Care for a beer?" I asked.

"Thanks," Alma said. She got a beer from the cooler. "It's awful hot in here."

"His electric's off," Sullivan said.

"I thought it was kind of weird you guys didn't have the game on," Alma said. "Billy's at home watching the game." She wandered off into the bedroom.

"Want to go over to Billy's house?" Sullivan asked. "We could take the beer."

"I'm not in the mood," I said.

Sullivan nodded. "I understand."

Three middle-aged women came up the steps and into the house without knocking. They stood frowning at me and Sullivan and the living room.

"Is this the sale?" the tallest woman asked.

"No," I said.

"I saw someone leaving with stuff," she said. "We thought there's supposed to be a sale here."

"They have some nice things," another woman said. "I wouldn't want that carpet, though."

"Huh-*uh*."

"Look at that sofa!"

The three women went on into the kitchen.

"I'm getting tired of this," I said. I got out of the recliner and went out on the steps and sat down. It was a little bit cooler outside, actually, though brighter. I had some sunglasses somewhere, thought I didn't remember where. In the car, maybe. Probably. Sullivan came out a moment or so later, carrying the cooler. He placed it on the grass in front of me and pulled out a couple of beers. He handed one to me. Then he closed the lid and sat down.

"You have to think of this as a new beginning," Sullivan said. "This is a time to grow. You're starting over."

A neighbor kid—he was from down the street, I think, I couldn't remember his name, he was just some kid—came around the corner of the house pushing my lawn mower.

"Hey!" I yelled. "Put that back."

The kid looked at me and blinked, wide-eyed and innocent. "Mom said I should get this before someone else did," he said.

I thought for a minute. Despite the dry summer, the grass was long and needed cutting.

"Okay," I said, "you can have the mower if you cut the grass first."

"That's the idea," Sullivan said. "You have to teach kids values."

The kid frowned at me, then shrugged and began pulling at the starter cord. The engine caught and the kid began pushing it quickly across the yard.

Two cars pulled up in front of the house and several women got out. They crossed the lawn and walked past me, up the steps and into the house. Alma Garcia came out of the house carrying a big bunch of things—some of Molly's clothes, one of my suits, a clock radio, and my shotgun.

"How much for all this?" she asked.

"The shotgun's not for sale," I said. The gun was in its vinyl case, and she was holding the case by the handle. I took it from her and handed it to Sullivan. "Here, you can have this."

"Really?" he asked.

"How come he gets the shotgun?" Alma asked.

"He's been helping," I said.

Alma saw the justice in that. "Well, how much for everything else?"

I shrugged. "Ten bucks."

"Oh, come on," she said. "I'll have to wash everything. How about eight?"

I shrugged again. "Whatever."

Alma slung my suit over her shoulder, struggling with all of Molly's clothes, and pulled some money from her jeans pocket. She was off balance and couldn't see what she had in her hand.

She said, "Here."

"I took the money and counted it. "That's nine," I said. I reached up and stuck the extra dollar back in her hand.

"Thanks," Alma said. She started down the steps. "I'll be back!" she said over her shoulder.

Sullivan had the shotgun out of the case and was admiring it.

"It's not that valuable a gun," I said. "I just saw it at a pawn shop one day and sort of bought it on impulse. It shoots good, though."

Sullivan placed the shotgun across his knees. "I really

appreciate this," he said. He reached over and touched me on the arm. "You know, I think you're going to come through all this just fine."

I shrugged, suddenly embarrassed. The kid pushed the lawnmower by us and sprayed the two of us with grass clippings. I covered my beer to keep grass out of it.

I said, "You know, she could have at least fed the dogs—or boarded them when she left."

"I know it," Sullivan said.

"And she could have paid the electric bill."

Sullivan said, "Yep."

Goddamn Molly.

A woman I had never seen before came out of the house carrying a big rattling box.

"How much?" she asked.

I said, "Let me see."

She set the box on the porch next to me and I looked over into it. Kitchen stuff, mostly—toaster, blender, coffee pot, a few plates and cups. But the deer skull was sitting on top.

"The deer skull's spoke for," I said.

"Spoke for?"

"Yep," I said. I took the skull and set it aside. "Ten bucks for everything else."

"I was gonna give that skull to my little boy. He likes stuff like that." The woman opened her billfold and pulled out a ten. "You know, you could make this a lot easier for everyone if you had everything marked."

"Next time I will," I said. I stuck the bill in my shirt pocket.

"Have a nice day," the woman said. She went down the steps and across the lawn carrying her box.

Sullivan stood up and leaned the shotgun against the house. He pulled two more beers from the cooler and closed the lid and sat back down. He handed me one of the beers. I hadn't yet opened the last one or finished the one before that.

"Thanks," I said.

I looked away from him, watching the woman carrying the box down the street. A car was pulling up in front of my house with a couple of women in it. Oh, what the hell. Everything was going. Was gone.

"Well—" I said, and stopped.

The kid with the lawnmower made another pass by us, gave us another shower of dirt and dried grass. The women in the car were getting out. One of them was looking at me.

"Well," I said. "What the hell. You might as well take the air conditioner, too."

Diane Wilson

Gone Shrimping

It was too bad Daddy had such a rocky thing going on with women because he needed a deckhand real bad and one of his girls would have to do. So he stood in his white undershirt with his hands on his hips and smoked his first cigarette as he carefully surveyed three sleeping girls. Female flesh and blood!

Recent experience had told Daddy that some girls wouldn't work no matter what he did or how many RC Colas he bought for the shrimping trip. They weren't in the mood that day. They were ticked off from the day before. Sharon Rose sure enough was on account of her eloping plan with Boudreaux being nixed so Daddy didn't even bother to go there even though he pretended he did and she pretended she was asleep. It was a mutual lying thing.

He shouted, "GET UP! One of you girls got exactly three minutes to get into my truck."

He meant me, of course. Not Sharon Rose, who was ticked off. Not Tammie Faye who was named after the wife of the famous TV evangelist, Jim Bakker, that Grandma listened to on her pink radio. Tammie Faye hated shrimp and that was a real problem in a shrimp-eating family. It started when Tammie Faye was five years old and Sharon Rose told her that shrimp crawled out of the bay, went up sewer pipes and nasty toilets, and bit people on the butt. Of course, Sharon Rose denied it, but Tammie Faye sure hated shrimp and it didn't matter if Momma boiled or fried them so light and fluffy that the shrimp flew out of her hot skillet.

She hated shrimp boats, too.

Three minutes were up! So I was the lucky dog that rolled over and fell out of bed. Good! Daddy had his deckhand! That little problem was done with. Then Daddy walked back into the kitchen and started giving Momma orders, something in addition to the three bacon and egg sandwiches on mayonnaise and white bread that he wanted. And the coffee. Don't forget the coffee! And his change of clean clothes!

I jumped into the truck as Daddy pitched a mason jar of coffee covered in newspaper into my lap and said, "Don't drink it!" That was my number one order. Don't drink the coffee. He drank the entire jar of coffee all by himself! Later on, he brewed a pot of coffee over the Coleman stove on the catch-all and I could drink all that I wanted. Six o'clock. Twelve o'clock. He didn't care. He had no problem with a twelve year old kid drinking a gallon of black coffee after midnight if she wanted to.

Daddy didn't say a word the entire ride to the bay. He didn't believe in talking with women or little girls except to give orders. What did they know? Something silly. That was okay with me. I was a nontalker. I missed geography lessons twice a week to take speech lessons from Mister HOW WING TON (try pitching that off your tongue) in the principal's office who said the least I could do was say his name.

Daddy didn't turn on the truck headlights even though they worked. They were the one thing that worked on his truck that was mainly a rusted pile of broke. The mirror and side door were stuck, the fenders were rusted out, and the tailgate was totally gone. Daddy had wired sack webbing across the entire back end to keep the net from rolling out.

Daddy didn't care about everyday stuff like how his truck looked or which girl was sitting in the truck with him.

As long as it was one of them! And if Daddy had any idea that one of his flesh and blood was a ticking time bomb fixing to go off in his house then he was Chicken Little's bestest friend. And he didn't even know Chicken Little. He didn't read children's books or talk to little kids or women who did.

So we coasted on moonlight (the exact same thing he'd do on his shrimp boat) because Daddy didn't need a headlight or a compass or a spotlight. He was a born sailor. Ask anybody at the bay. Give Daddy the moon and the wind and he'd wind up within two feet of where he wanted to go. He had a lot of information to keep in his head. Shrimp and the water and what time of day it was and what the moon was doing so Daddy wrote notes on the cabin wall of his boat.

Northeast corner of Mesquite Bay.

Full moon and scattered shrimp.

Some shrimpers kept a logbook and penciled in their coordinates, but not Daddy. He kept it simple. Write on the cabin wall and for god's sake, nobody better paint over it!

There was another reason for no headlights and it was the same reason gillnetters didn't park in front of their skiffs, but across the harbor or in front of a shrimp boat that wasn't going out. Game wardens. There was one living in the next town over and he had a nasty habit of showing up. Daddy said no sense in stirring up trouble.

But the minute we hit the docks, forget everything about game wardens and leaving early and being quiet. Daddy was changing shrimp nets. That old chain net he put on yesterday wouldn't work on opening day of shrimp season. What was he thinking? He needed his secret bottomless net that was rolled up on top of the cabin. That net snuck up on shrimp like nobody's business.

So for half an hour, we worked like crazy in the dark, counting lengths of chain and unhooking and re-hooking net thimbles so many times that I got confused which side was right and which side was left and besides it was dark as heck and I couldn't see anything, so Daddy came over and re-did the end of the net I was working on.

Some nets just didn't work. Not in the mood that day. Maybe they were ticked off because a shrimper had drugged them through a muddy dredge hole! I sure the heck would be mad. Mud from a dredge hole took the hide off your fingers and every touch of your finger left a trail of blood. Mud would eat a net, too. Leave a muddy net in the sun for two days and watch it disappear.

But Daddy was extremely nice to his nets. He said to treat them right and they'll treat him right. So he shook every croaker and ribbonfish out of his net and when he was done with that, he'd drag it an extra mile to wash the seaweed and mud out of it. I could cook a meal on daddy's deck or sleep in the webbing. Once, though, he drug too close to the docks and a roaming game warden accused him of dragging his net in a closed area of the bay and no amount of arguing on Daddy's part would convince the game warden otherwise. In his law book, shrimpers were outlaws.

Three cups of coffee and a half a pack of Camel cigarettes later, Daddy revved the dead engine alive and nosed the boat into the wind. He kissed that dock goodbye and the goodbye didn't come fast enough.

Participant Bios

Dorothy Ellis Barnett graduated from The University of Texas at Austin with a BA in Anthropology, an MA in English, and a James A. Michener Fellowship. She is professor emerita in English and Creative Writing at Austin Community College, where she taught for over 20 years. She earned an MFA from Pacific Lutheran University in her sixties while conquering breast cancer.

Pamela Booton is a longtime Austin resident, arts advocate, and financial consultant. She serves as director of the Alamo Bay Writers' Workshop and Alamo Bay Press. Co-editor of the *Amazing Imagination Vacation,* project manager for the oral history documentary *Seadrift Fishermen Legacy Project,* and organizer of the *Texas Louisiana Gulf Coast Shindig,* Pamela lives in Austin with her husband Javier VanWisse and their two dachshunds, Rudy and Grady.

Linda Caplin is writing her memoir of a life full of adventure and joy. From her travels as a Peace Corps Volunteer in Ecuador to a career as a counselor at Austin Community College, and now to reflection by the pool with kids, grandkids and four legged kids, Linda shares a life well lived.

After a rewarding corporate career in Dallas, **Linda Dane** retired to the beautiful Texas coastal town of Palo Alto, where she spends her time writing, reading, and watching the orangest sunrises in Texas.

Gracie Fleming spent her childhood in a place where the land turns from desert to ranch and farmland and springs feed a beautiful river that Mexicans call Bravo and Americans call Grande. It's something of an oasis where locals keep secrets, travelers trade stories, and magic abounds. Those stories, secrets, and magic color the novels, stories, and poetry she writes.

Lee Meitzen Grue is a New Orleans poet and fiction writer whose work celebrates New Orleans culture and music. Her published books include *Trains and Other Intrusions: Poems*; F*rench Quarter Poems*; *In the Sweet Balance of the Flesh*; and *Goodbye, Silver, Silver Cloud*; and *Downtown*. The recipient of an NEA Fellowship, she is the longtime editor of *The New Laurel Review*.

A native of California who has lived in Austin, Texas for 31 years, **Gina Harlow** blogs about food and gardening at *Peaches and Prsciuotto* and is at work on a memoir.

Julie Jean-Marie Jewert Johnson-Jones is mother of five and grandmother of five. She wants to be able to write down everything she thinks about or goes through with the goal of helping someone with her words, to "touch someone the way so many wonderful people have touched me...."

A retired community college counselor from Austin, Texas, **Diane Kramer** is working on a collection of essays about the kindnesses that people do for others called *Humanity Rides the Bus*. Diane is also a guest blogger at *Peace Through Pie*.

Kathryn Lane writes both fiction and poetry. Her fiction has been published in *New Border Voices: An Anthology; Swirl Literary Journal; ¡Arriba Baseball!* and *ABWW13*. Originally from Mexico, her writing is often inspired by Latin American cultures. She performs poetry in both English and Spanish. Her new novel, *Barefoot Park,* will be published in 2016.

Dr. Barbara Lewis is Professor of English and Assistant Dean of Academic Departments at Austin Community College. She received her PhD from University of Southern California. Proud mother of four, grandmother of thirteen, and great grandmother of seventeen, Dr. Lewis lives near Austin, Texas. Dr. Lewis recently published the first volume of her memoir, *Sherrod Village.* She is working on her autobiographty *Woman, Wild.*

Bobby Lindsey was born in Seadrift, Texas and graduated from Midwestern State University. He owned a private investigation agency in Dallas, was a field producer for NBC News in Europe, was Baseball Coach at International High School Frankfurt, Germany, and was International Scout for Cincinnati Reds baseball team.

Jay Minton is a passionate sound designer, composer, musician, art director, web designer and Jack of all trades. He has worked as a production sound recordist in Thailand, Bali, Cambodia, and all over the United States.

Aubrey Parker is a painter, sculptor, and songwriter from Bexar County, Texas. Living on on Keller Bay in Olivia, Texas, he remains active in the arts and community, building and riding motorcycles and restoring old cars. He is the manager and curator of the Seadrift Art Boat.

Sophie Rousmaniere has worked as a filmmaker and freelance journalist in the US, Canada, India, Indonesia, Mexico, Guatemala, Pakistan, Laos, Vietnam and Thailand. She has produced, edited and directed over thirty documentaries, short films and music videos.

The art of **Reji Thomas** is held in private collections and in public places around the world. Clients include the State Capitol of Texas Restorations, Democratic National Convention, Ann Richards, Barbara Jordan, B.B. King, as well as many corporate headquarters, colleges, and universities. Reji Thomas continues to produce brilliant art and support Austin creativity.

Seadrift resident **Janie Waghorne**, community leader, wife, mother, grandmother, and traveler, hosted the Alamo Bay Writers' Workshop Seadrift 2014 poetry class in her magic garden on San Antonio Bay.

Born in Plaquemine, Louisiana, **Dr. Hazel Ward** has been the recipient of many awards and honors, including a Woodrow Wilson fellowship and a Ford Foundation grant. Dr. Ward has taught English at colleges and universities throughout the Austin and Houston area, and is reired Dean of Communications at Austin Community College.

Lowell Mick White is the author the novels *Professed* and *That Demon Life*, and of the story collection *Long Time Ago Good.* He is Editor of Alamo Bay Press.

The author of *An Unreasonable Woman,* **Diane Wilson** is a fourth-generation shrimper who began fishing the bays off the Texas Gulf Coast when she was eight. Her fight for the environment and for justice has won her a number of awards, including the National Fisherman Magazine Award and Mother Jones's Hell Raiser of the Month.

Books from

ALAMO BAY PRESS

www.alamobaypress.com

The Cowtown Circle

by Dave Oliphant
ISBN: 978-0990863212

Dave Oliphant's thirteenth book of poetry, *The Cowtown Circle,* is divided into six sections, moving from an eclectic gathering of poems devoted to nature, topical issues, and the imprisonment of captured WWII German soldiers in Hearne, Texas, to a section of María Poems (a series begun in 1976) and to sections on grandchildren and a visit to New York City, on music (classical, jazz, and Indian), on U.S. Presidents, and on a group of modernist Texas artists active during the Second World War.

Like That: New and Selected Poems

by Sybil Pittman Estess
ISBN: 978-0990863229

In this poetry collection, **Sybil Pittman Estess** takes readers on an intensely personal journey, a deep exploration of life in contemporary America. "These are poems of witness," says 2008 Texas Poet Laureate Larry Thomas. "...of witness to a life fully lived, of witness to birth, friendship, death, and the unforgiving pain of loss; and of witness to a world rife with the wounds of global warming, the violence of guns, yet a world still teeming with transient beauty."

Art Stronger Than Hate!

by Issa Nyaphaga
ISBN: 978-0990863243

In **Issa Nyaphaga**'s new book, *Art Stronger Than Hate!,* the former artist for the French magazine Charlie Hebdo offers a visual commentary on our current political, social, and economic world, arguing for Free Speech rather than Hate Speech. *Art Stronger Than Hate!* offers evidence that art can save lives and inspire the human spirit.

Blood at the Root

by Lee Meitzen Grue
ISBN: 978-0990863229

Set in Southern Louisiana, **Lee Grue**'s *Blood at the Root* is a fly-on-the wall look at an aspect of New Orleans culture that borders magic, imagination, sex, telling the festinating tale of Camilla Jane, High John the Conqueror, and Creeping Jesus, and the sisterly bonds that stretch beyond death.

For Mr. Raindrinker

by Ken Fontenot
ISBN: 978-0990863274

In this novel, **Ken Fontenot** introduces readers to Kent Soileau, who lives an upside-down life as a professional job-hopper and as an inmate of a nut house. He has assembled an impressive resume of diverse and comical experiences, from being a driver for Mississippi River-boat pilots, to a French Quarter bartender, to a genetics research associate. Kent is a true searcher, whether searching for food, a place to stay, happiness—or the meaning of life.

www.alamobaypress.com

www.ingramcontent.com/pod-product-compliance
Lightning Source LLC
Chambersburg PA
CBHW061126100726
47911CB00013B/691
* 9 7 8 0 9 9 0 8 6 3 2 6 7 *

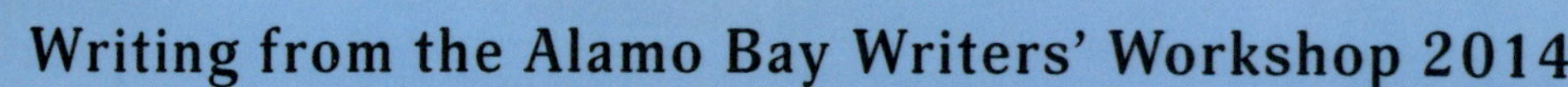

Writing from the Alamo Bay Writers' Workshop 2014

Few experiences have had the profound impact on my writing as the Alamo Bay Writers' Workshop in Seadrift, Texas. Writers Mick White and Diane Wilson together with poet Lee Meitzen Grue presented outdoor lectures at the harbor amid the waters of San Antonio Bay and in nearby tranquil gardens where they inspired us with the passion, love and dedication that moves their creative work. In this Texas commercial fishing town, all three authors and Pamela Booton, Director of Alamo Bay Press, took us on a journey beyond the written and spoken word to indulge all of our senses with food, music and art.

—Kathryn Lane, author of *Barefoot Park*

I am anchored in Seadrift near a very salty sea where there is intuition excluding rationality, dreams excluding language, and mysteries excluding a clanking, cranky world. I am a borderline mystic, a tad unsociable, and happy as a clam.

—Diane Wilson, author of *An Unreasonable Woman*

ALAMO BAY PRESS
SEADRIFT • AUSTIN

ISBN 978-0-9908632-6-7
51595
9 780990 863267